SCIENCE LIBRARY

PLANET EARTH

SCIENCE LIBRARY

PLANET EARTH

John Farndon
Consultant: Sue Becklake

Miles Kelly PUBLISHING

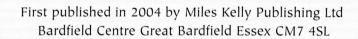

First published in 2004 by Miles Kelly Publishing Ltd
Bardfield Centre Great Bardfield Essex CM7 4SL

2 4 6 8 10 9 7 5 3 1

British Library Cataloguing-in-Publication Data
A catalogue record for this book is available from the British Library

ISBN 1-84236-283-6

Printed in China

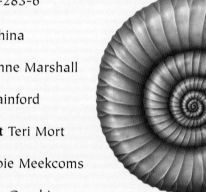

Editorial Director Anne Marshall

Editor Jenni Rainford

Editorial Assistant Teri Mort

Design Concept Debbie Meekcoms

Design Stonecastle Graphics

Copy Editor Rosalind Beckman

Consultant Sue Becklake

Proofreader Hayley Kerr

Indexer Hilary Bird

www.mileskelly.net
info@mileskelly.net

Contents

How to use this book

PLANET EARTH is packed with information, colour photos, diagrams, illustrations and features to help you learn more about science. Do you know what makes a volcano erupt or how the Moon affects tides? Did you know about the dangers of pollution or how hot the Sun's surface is? Enter the fascinating world of science and learn about why things happen, where things come from and how things work. Find out how to use this book and start your journey of scientific discovery.

Main text
Each page begins with an introduction to the different subject areas.

The grid
The pages have a background grid. Pictures and captions sit on the grid and have unique co-ordinates. By using the grid references, you can move from page to page and find out more about related topics.

To scale
Some pages show the size of an object in relation to another so that you can compare how big or small things really are.

20

Mountain high

MOUNTAINS LOOK solid and unchanging, but they are being built up, then worn away by the weather, all the time. The world's highest mountains were actually formed quite recently in the Earth's history. The Himalayas, for instance, were built up in the last 40 million years, and are still growing, even today. The most ancient mountain ranges have long been worn flat, or reduced to hills, such as New York's Adirondacks, which are now over 1 billion years old.

▶ Three types of mountain range.

Read further › formation of volcanoes
▶▶ pg23 (b22)

Neat folds
A few mountains, such as Washington's Mount St Helens, are volcanoes – tall cones built up by successive eruptions of lava and ash. Most, however, are thrown up by the immense power of the Earth's crust moving. Some are huge slabs called fault blocks, or 'horst', caused by powerful earthquakes. But all the world's great mountain ranges, such as the Andes and Rockies, were made by the crumpling of rock layers as tectonic plates pushed against each other. Such mountains are called fold mountains.

Volcanic peak

Fold mountain

To scale
Each square = 1000 m
The highest mountains – measured from sea level to summit – in each continent, to scale

Jayakusuma (Oceania) 5030 m

Elbrus (Europe) 5642 m

Kilimanjaro (Africa) 5895 m

Mt McKinley (North America) 6194 m

Aconcagua (South America) 6960 m

Mount Everest is growing slightly taller every year by a few millimetres

1 2 3 4 5 6 7 8 9 10 11 12 13 14 15 16

Main image
Each topic is clearly illustrated. Some images are labelled, providing further information.

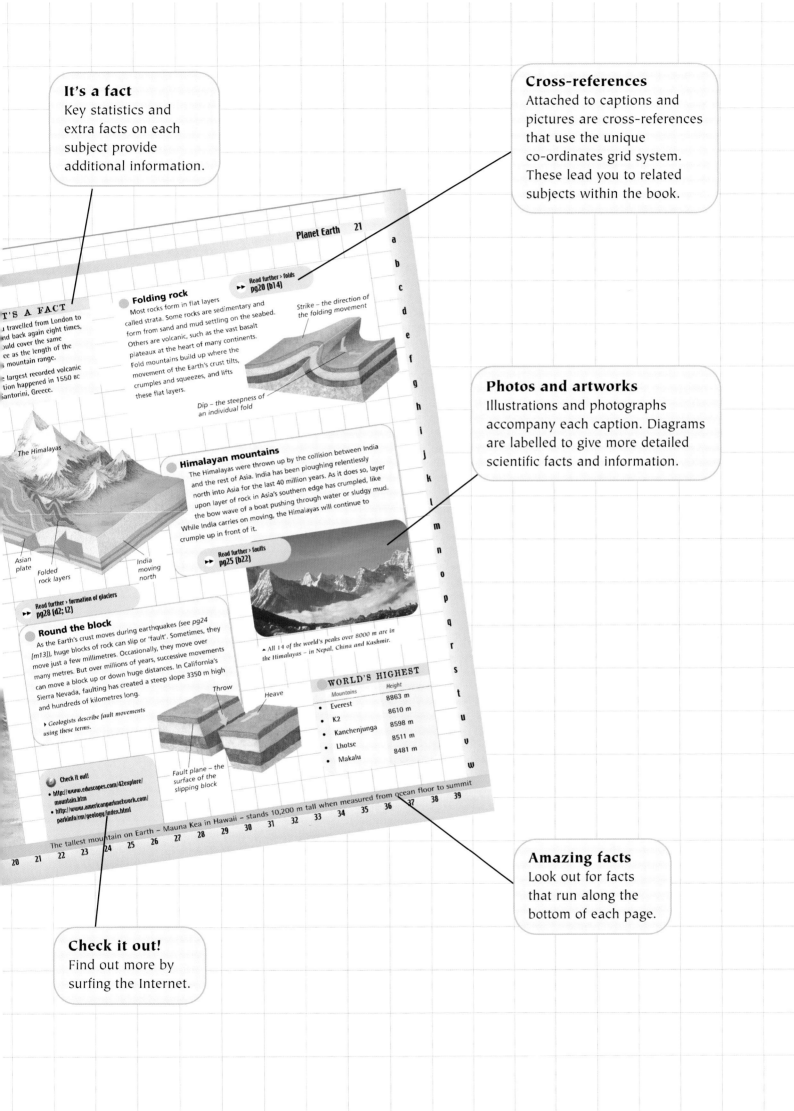

It's a fact
Key statistics and extra facts on each subject provide additional information.

Cross-references
Attached to captions and pictures are cross-references that use the unique co-ordinates grid system. These lead you to related subjects within the book.

Read further › folds
►► pg20 (b14)

Folding rock
Most rocks form in flat layers called strata. Some rocks are sedimentary and form from sand and mud settling on the seabed. Others are volcanic, such as the vast basalt plateaux at the heart of many continents. Fold mountains build up where the movement of the Earth's crust tilts, crumples and squeezes, and lifts these flat layers.

Strike – the direction of the folding movement

Dip – the steepness of an individual fold

IT'S A FACT
...u travelled from London to ...nd back again eight times, ...uld cover the same ...ce as the length of the ...s mountain range.

...e largest recorded volcanic ...tion happened in 1550 BC ...Santorini, Greece.

Photos and artworks
Illustrations and photographs accompany each caption. Diagrams are labelled to give more detailed scientific facts and information.

The Himalayas

Himalayan mountains
The Himalayas were thrown up by the collision between India and the rest of Asia. India has been ploughing relentlessly north into Asia for the last 40 million years. As it does so, layer upon layer of rock in Asia's southern edge has crumpled, like the bow wave of a boat pushing through water or sludgy mud. While India carries on moving, the Himalayas will continue to crumple up in front of it.

Read further › faults
►► pg25 (b22)

Asian plate
Folded rock layers
India moving north

Read further › formation of glaciers
►► pg28 (d2; l2)

Round the block
As the Earth's crust moves during earthquakes (see pg24 [m13]), huge blocks of rock can slip or 'fault'. Sometimes, they move just a few millimetres. Occasionally, they move over many metres. But over millions of years, successive movements can move a block up or down huge distances. In California's Sierra Nevada, faulting has created a steep slope 3350 m high and hundreds of kilometres long.

▸ Geologists describe fault movements using these terms.

▲ All 14 of the world's peaks over 8000 m are in the Himalayas – in Nepal, China and Kashmir.

Throw
Heave

WORLD'S HIGHEST
Mountains	Height
• Everest	8863 m
• K2	8610 m
• Kanchenjunga	8598 m
• Lhotse	8511 m
• Makalu	8481 m

Check it out!
• http://www.eduscapes.com/42explore/mountain.htm
• http://www.americanparknetwork.com/parkinfo/rm/geology/index.html

Fault plane – the surface of the slipping block

The tallest mountain on Earth – Mauna Kea in Hawaii – stands 10,200 m tall when measured from ocean floor to summit

20 21 22 23 24 25 26 27 28 29 30 31 32 33 34 35 36 37 38 39

a b c d e f g h i j k l m n o p q r s t u v w

Amazing facts
Look out for facts that run along the bottom of each page.

Check it out!
Find out more by surfing the Internet.

The jewel planet

THE EARTH is one of nine planets in the Solar System that orbit (circle) the Sun. Like some of the other planets, it is a big ball of rock, wrapped around with a thin layer of gases, called the atmosphere (see pg32 [i18]). Yet the Earth is different from the other planets in crucial ways. From a distance, it looks like a blue-and-green jewel hanging in space. It is partly blue because, uniquely among the planets, the Earth has huge amounts of water in oceans (see pg31 [q25]). It is partly green because, unlike other planets, the water supports life.

►► **Read further › tectonic plates**
pg24 (d2); pg25 (b22)

● **Inside the Earth**

The Earth is not a solid ball. Vibrations from earthquakes (see pg24 [k13]) and volcanic explosions (see pg22 [o11]) have revealed a complex internal structure. Around the outside is a thin rocky shell or crust, between 6 and 40 km thick. Beneath the crust is a thick mantle of rock so hot that it flows like treacle, only very, very much slower. The mantle is about 2900 km thick. Beneath it, there is a core of metal (mostly iron and nickel). The outer core is so hot it is always molten; the inner core at the very centre of the Earth is solid because pressures are so great it cannot melt, despite top temperatures of over 7000°C.

Crust

Mantle

Outer core

Inner core

Continents (see pg16 [r16])

● **View from above**

From space, it is clear just how much of the Earth is covered by oceans – nearly three-quarters of its surface (see pg31 [q25]). Emerging above the oceans are seven masses of land (see pg16 [s16]). These are the continents of North and South America, Oceania, Antarctica, Africa, Asia and Europe, plus many thousands of islands, of all different sizes – some no bigger than a small rock.

Temperatures at the centre of the Earth are hotter than on the Sun's surface

IT'S A FACT

• The centre of the Earth is 6378 km below the surface.

• The Earth weighs about 6000 trillion trillion tonnes.

◄ *Viewed from space, swirls of cloud, the oceans and continents are visible on the Earth.*

Seas
(see pg31 [d29])

Atmosphere
(see pg32 [i18])

►► **Read further › early Earth / age of the Earth / radioactive dating**
pg14 (h16; n2); pg15 (b22)

Space rock

The Earth has not always existed – it formed gradually over time *(see pg14 [p10])*. Radioactive dating (the study of atoms and their radioactive rays) has shown that the oldest meteorites – large rocks from space – that crashed down into the Earth are about 4.5 billion years old. From this, scientists have worked out that this is probably how old the Earth is. Meteorites are made from rock and iron, just like the Earth, and originated around the same time. In fact, the Earth was probably created by the collision of masses of meteorites.

►► **Read further › Earth's composition**
pg18 (d2; n12)

Composition of the Earth

Most of the Earth is made from just four chemical elements: iron, oxygen, silicon and magnesium. Much of its rocky crust is made from combinations of two of these elements; oxygen and silicon, known as silicates. But there are small quantities of many other elements, such as aluminium and calcium. The various ways these elements combine mean that the Earth's crust contains many different materials.

Sulphur 2.7%
Calcium 0.6%
Nickel 2.7%
Aluminium 0.4%
Magnesium 13%
Others 0.6%
Silicon 17%
Iron 35%
Oxygen 28%

DOWN TO EARTH

• The Earth is not perfectly round. It bulges at the Equator (the middle), making it slightly tangerine-shaped.

• The diameter of the Earth at the Equator is 12,756 km, but only 12,712 km at the North and South Poles.

◄ *A meteorite crashing into the Earth. The meteorite penetrates through the Earth's atmosphere and reaches the ground.*

🌐 **Check it out!**

• http://www.enchantedlearning. com/subjects/astronomy/planets /earth/Inside.shtml

• http://sse.jpl.nasa.gov/features /planets/earth/earth.html

• http://stardate.org/resources/ ssguide/earth.html

The study of the shape of the Earth is called geodesy

a b c d e f g h i j k l m n o p q r s t u v w

Spinning globe

THOUGH IT seems perfectly still, the Earth is actually spinning around at an average speed of over 1600 km/h. It is also hurtling through the darkness of space on its journey around the Sun at over 100,000 km/h. We are unaware of this rapid movement because we are locked firmly to the ground by gravity. But as the Earth spins and whirls through space, the view of the Sun from different places on the Earth is constantly changing, bringing not only day and night but all the seasons, too.

IT'S A FACT

• During each orbit of the Sun, the Earth travels a distance of more than 939,886,400 km.

• The Earth's distance from the Sun is about 150 million km.

• Climate is affected by sunspots – dark patches on the Sun.

Earth lit having turned towards the Sun

◄ *This satellite image shows half the Earth is exposed to the Sun at any time. Radiation from the Sun is the Earth's main source of energy. This provides huge amounts of both heat and light, without which there would be no life on Earth.*

Day and night

At any one time, half the Earth is facing towards the Sun and is brightly lit, while the other half is facing away from the Sun and is in darkness. As the Earth turns while the Sun stays still, the dark and sunlit halves move around the world, bringing day and night to different parts. Because the Earth turns eastwards, we see the Sun rising in the east as the Earth turns our part of the world towards it, and setting in the west as it turns us away from the Sun. The Earth turns completely around once every 24 hours, which is why there are 24 hours in every day.

Earth in darkness having turned away from the Sun

 Check it out!

• http://www.enchantedlearning.com/subjects/astronomy/planets/earth/Seasons.shtml
• http://www.hexadyne.com/Educational/Science/4seasons.html
• http://kids.msfc.nasa.gov/News/2000/News-AutumnalEquinox.asp

DOWN TO EARTH

• As the Earth spins around every 24 hours, places near the poles barely move at all, while places at the Equator whizz around at over 1600 km/h.

• The Earth takes 0.242 days longer than a calendar year to complete its orbit. To make up for this, an extra day is added to the end of February every four years. This is called a leap year.

The Moon is putting a brake on the Earth's rotation, slowing it by two-thousandths of 1 second every century

a
b
c
d
e
f
g
h
i
j
k
l
m
n
o
p
q
r
s
t
u
v
w

▼ *The world's 24 time zones.*

Yearly journey

►► **Read further › Sun's heat**
pg13 (c31)

The Earth's orbit around the Sun takes 365.242 days, which is why there are 365 days in a calendar year. Since the orbit is not a perfect circle but an ellipse (oval), the Earth is closer to the Sun at some points than others. Its closest point, called the perihelion, occurs on 3 January; its furthest point, called the aphelion, occurs on 4 July.

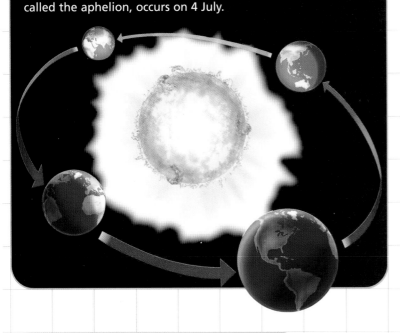

Time around the world

As the Earth rotates, the Sun rises in one place and sets in another. So that noon is always at the middle of the day, the world is divided into 24 time zones, one for each hour of the day. You put your clock forward 1 hour for each zone you pass through as you travel east; or behind 1 hour for each time zone as you travel west. So at noon in London, it is 7 a.m. in New York or 8 p.m. in Tokyo.

►► **Read further › time zones**
pg10 (m2)

All the seasons

The Earth does not spin upright, but is tilted at an angle, which always remains the same. When the Earth is on one side of the Sun, and the northern hemisphere (the world north of the Equator) is tilted towards it, it receives more sun, bringing summer. At the same time, the southern hemisphere is tilted away from the Sun, bringing winter. When Earth is on the other side of the Sun and the northern hemisphere is tilted away, winter occurs. In between, as the Earth moves around the Sun and neither hemisphere is tilted more towards it, we have spring and autumn.

Northern hemisphere is tilted away from the Sun – winter

Southern hemisphere is tilted towards the Sun – summer

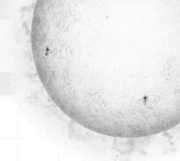

►► **Read further › climate patterns**
pg12 (p2); pg13 (b22)

Warm and cold

THE NEARER a place is to the Equator, the warmer the weather, or climate, tends to be. At the Equator, the Sun climbs high in the sky so its rays are warm. Away from the Equator, the Sun climbs less high, so its rays give less warmth. At the North and South Poles, the Sun is so low, it gives very little warmth at all. The effect is to give the world three broad climate bands either side of the Equator: the warm tropics, the cold polar regions, and a moderate 'temperate' zone in between.

Temperate grassland (prairie and steppe)

Cool conifer forest (taiga)

North Pole

Equator

South Pole

Temperate deciduous woodland

Dry temperate

Tropical grassland

Mountainous

Climate patterns

The warmth of a region's climate depends on how close it is to the Equator. But oceans and mountain ranges have a huge influence too, so the pattern of climate is complicated, with many local variations. Coastal areas tend to be damper and cooler, for instance, while continental interiors far inland tend to be drier and more extreme, with hot summers and cold winters. Antarctica has the coldest climate. It is so cold that almost nothing grows and nobody lives there.

Tropical forest

Desert

Polar and tundra

Because of global warming, Arctic Sea ice is 40 per cent thinner than it was 40 years ago

Warm tropics

The tropics are very warm, with temperatures averaging over 27°C all year round. But the tropical climate is varied. Some tropical places are warm and dry, including hot deserts such as the Sahara; some are warm and wet; and others have marked wet and dry seasons. Where it is wet in the tropics, it tends to be very wet indeed, since the warm air takes up huge amounts of moisture. Large thunderclouds often build up in the morning heat, then unleash torrents of rain in the afternoon (see pg35 [q29]). Steamy rainforests flourish in this hot, moist climate.

▸ *The Amazon rainforest in South America has more species of plants and animals than anywhere else on Earth.*

▶▶ **Read further › seasons**
pg11 [m22]

▶▶ **Read further › ozone layer / atmosphere / pressure**
pg13 (n22); pg32 (l2); pg33 (j22)

Global warming

When heat from the Sun reaches the Earth, some of it penetrates the atmosphere and reaches the ground. Much of this heat is then reflected back into space. Certain gases in the air trap heat reflected from the ground, rather like the glass in a greenhouse. In the past, this natural 'greenhouse effect' has kept the Earth comfortably warm. But the gases pumped into the air by the burning of coal and oil in factories and cars, for example, have trapped much more heat. Scientists believe that this is causing global (worldwide) warming of the climate, which could have devastating effects.

Heat trapped inside the atmosphere by greenhouse gases

Rays turned away by the atmosphere

Rays from the Sun

Heat reaching the Earth's surface

Trashing the Earth

In recent years, human activity has posed an increasing threat to the Earth's fragile resources, damaging everything from the atmosphere to animal life. Car exhausts and industrial plants are choking the air and turning rain acidic. Gases from supersonic jets and refrigerators are punching a hole in the world's protective ozone layer. Farming chemicals poison rivers. Unique species of animals and plants are vanishing for ever. Forests are being felled, vast areas of countryside are being buried under concrete and beautiful marine environments are being gradually destroyed.

▸ *Dangers to the world's climate caused by human activity.*

▶▶ **Read further › global warming**
pg13 (c31); pg32 (l2); pg33 (j22)

Siberia has become 5°C warmer over the last 30 years

Earth story

THE STORY of the Earth began about 4.6 billion years ago when dust whirling around the newborn Sun started to clump into lumps of rock called planetesimals. Then, pulled together by their mutual gravity, the planetesimals clumped together to form the Earth and other planets. Soon after, a giant rock crashed into the Earth so violently that the rock melted, splashed off and cooled to become the Moon. The Earth was so shaken by the impact that all the elements in it separated. The dense metals, iron and nickel, collapsed to the centre to form its core, while lighter materials formed the Earth's rocky crust.

● DOWN TO EARTH

• Fossils only indicate to geologists whether the rock in which they are found is relatively old or young.

• Radioactive dating works because after rocks form, certain atoms break down at a steady rate, sending out rays or radioactivity. By assessing how many atoms in the rock have changed, geologists can work out its age.

● Early Earth

A mass of erupting volcanoes and smoke appeared when the Earth was formed. Streams of lava (molten rock) turned the Earth's surface into churning, red-hot oceans. Huge gas bubbles rose from the interior and belched out through the volcanoes to form a thick, cloudy – and highly poisonous – atmosphere. Eventually, as the Earth began to cool, a crust formed around the Earth as the lava oceans hardened.

▶▶ Read further > rocks / volcanoes
pg18 (n12); pg22 (d2)

▼ *The steam and gas that billowed from volcanoes formed the Earth's poisonous atmosphere.*

● In the beginning

When the Earth first formed, it was little more than a red-hot ball. But over half a billion years, it gradually cooled down and, slowly, a hard crust of rock began to form. An atmosphere containing poisonous gases, such as methane, hydrogen and ammonia, soon wrapped around the planet, rising from fierce volcanoes on the surface *(see pg22 [p11])*. After about 1 billion years, the air began to clear as water vapour that had gathered in the clouds fell as rain, to create the oceans, flooding basins in the Earth's crust to form continents.

▶▶ Read further > volcanoes / oceans
pg22 (n2); pg30 (d2)

The oldest known rocks are the Acasta gneiss rocks in Canada – they are 3.9 billion years old

Ages of the Earth

▶▶ Read further › rock weathering
pg19 (h30)

Layers of rock tend to form one on top of another, so the oldest is usually at the bottom. The order of layers from top to bottom is known as the geological column. Even if the layers have been disturbed, it is often possible to work out the order in which they formed. Because different plants and animals lived at different times in the Earth's past, experts can date a layer of rock by the fossils it contains. Using these clues, they have built up a picture of the successive rock layers. This way, they have divided the last 590 million years of the Earth's history into 12 units of time called Periods, each lasting many millions of years.

Quaternary Period: *0–2 mya*
Many mammals die out; humans evolve

Tertiary Period: *2–65 mya*
First large mammals appear; birds thrive; grasslands spread

Cretaceous Period: *65–144 mya*
Dinosaurs die out; first flowering plants

Jurassic Period: *144–213 mya*
Age of the dinosaurs; some dinosaurs evolve into birds

Triassic Period: *213–248 mya*
Mammals and seed-bearing plants appear

Permian Period: *248–286 mya*
Conifers appear, but many animals die out as deserts spread

Carboniferous Period: *286–360 mya*
Reptiles evolve; vast areas of swampy fern forests

Devonian Period: *360–408 mya*
Insects and amphibians evolve; ferns and mosses as big as trees

Silurian Period: *408–438 mya*
Plants appear on land and fish in rivers

Ordovician Period: *438–505 mya*
Sahara is covered in ice; fish-like creatures evolve in the sea

Cambrian Period: *505–590 mya*
No life on land but shellfish thrive in the oceans

Precambrian Time: *Before 590 mya*
First micro-organisms appear and give atmosphere the oxygen that larger animals need to breathe

▲ *Timeline showing the Earth's formation millions of years ago (mya) plus layers of rock built up through the ages.*

• If all the Earth's history were crammed into the hours of one day, humans would appear less than 2 minutes before midnight!

• The oxygen most animals need to be able to breathe was put into the air by minute plants in the sea, called cyanobacteria, over billions of years.

Fossil record

The first signs of life on the Earth – probably tiny bacteria – appeared almost 4 billion years ago. But the first animals with shells and bones emerged less than 600 million years ago. Some have been preserved as fossils – over time their hard remains have turned to stone. With the help of fossils like the ammonite shellfish, geologists have built up a detailed picture of the Earth's history.

▲ *The ammonite's body was covered by a spiral shell. The body rotted while the shell became a fossil.*

🌐 **Check it out!**

• http://www.kidscosmos.org/kid-stuff/kids-basalt-history.html

Most of Earth's water probably came from ice in comets that hit the planet in its early days

Moving continents

SLOWLY, SLOWLY, the Earth's surface is moving around beneath our feet all the time. Look at a map of the world and you will see, for example, that the west coast of Africa looks as if it would slot into the east coast of South America like pieces of a jigsaw. The reason is that 220 million years ago – just before the age of the dinosaurs – they were actually joined together. In fact, all the world's continents were joined together then, in one huge landmass that geologists call Pangaea. Pangaea gradually split up into today's continents as plate movements caused earthquakes. The continents drifted to where they are today (continental drift) and are still moving!

● IT'S A FACT

• New York is moving about 2.5 cm further away from London every year.

• On average, continents move at the same rate as fingernails grow – about 2 mm every month.

• Some tectonic plates have moved so far, they have travelled half way around the globe.

▶▶ **Read further › earthquakes pg25 (b22)**

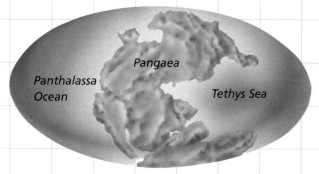

220 million years ago (mya) there was just one giant land mass, called Pangaea (meaning 'all Earth'), and one giant ocean, known as Panthalassa. But a long arm of the ocean, the Tethys Sea, stretched into the heart of Pangaea

200 mya Pangaea split either side of the Tethys Sea. To the north was Laurasia, including North America, Europe and most of Asia. To the south was Gondwanaland, including South America, Africa, Australia, Antarctica and India

135 mya the South Atlantic Ocean opened up between the continents of Africa and South America. India then broke off from Africa and drifted towards Asia. Europe and North America were still joined at this time

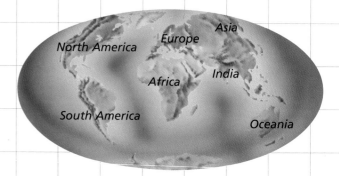

Today North America and Europe are widely separated, having split 60 million years ago. India has crunched into Asia, Australia is moving into the tropics and Antarctica has moved to the South Pole

Tectonic plates only formed about 500 million years after the Earth's hard shell (lithosphere) became thick enough

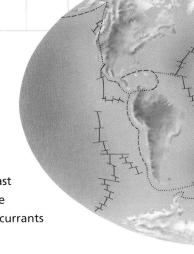

▲ *The jagged boundaries between the plates of the Earth's surface.*

The world's biggest plates

It is not just the continents that are moving – so are the ocean beds. In fact, the whole of the Earth's surface is on the move. Its rigid outer shell of rock is split into about 20 giant slabs called tectonic plates: nine huge ones and about 12 smaller ones. These plates are constantly on the move, slipping past each other, and jostling this way and that. The continents are embedded in these plates like currants in a bun, and move with them.

Key

——— Plate boundaries pulling apart
– – – Plate boundaries pushing together
·········· Plate boundaries sliding past each other

▶▶ **Read further › fault lines**
pg21 (o22)

Plates pushing together

In some places, tectonic plates are crunching together. Where this happens, one of the plates – typically the one carrying a continent – rides over the other and forces it down into the Earth's interior. This process is called subduction. Where one plate dives beneath the other, there is often a deep trench in the ocean floor *(see pg30 [q10])*.

▼ *One plate being pushed beneath another.*

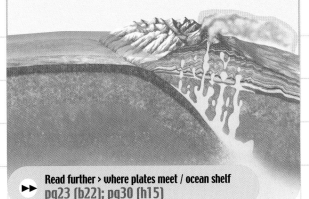

▶▶ **Read further › where plates meet / ocean shelf**
pg23 (b22); pg30 (h15)

DOWN TO EARTH

• One sign that continents have moved is the discovery of fossils of tropical ferns in the Arctic and tropical reptiles in Antarctica!

• Many of the same dinosaurs were found in both Europe and North America. This is because the continents were joined together until the dinosaurs died out, about 65 million years ago.

Plates moving apart

In some places, usually in the mid-ocean on the seabed, tectonic plates move apart or diverge. As they move apart, hot molten magma *(see pg22 [w11])* from the Earth's interior wells up through the gap and solidifies on the exposed edges. So the seabed grows wider and wider. The floor of the Pacific Ocean is becoming wider by about 20 cm every year.

▼ *Two plates moving apart (diverging) under the ocean.*

▶▶ **Read further › where plates diverge**
pg20 (b14); pg24 (d2); pg30 (h15)

Check it out!
• http://kids.earth.nasa.gov/archive/pangaea/
• http://www.enchantedlearning.com/subjects/dinosaurs/glossary/Contdrift.shtml

In 150 million years' time, southern California will be next to Alaska

Rocks and minerals

ROCKS ARE the hard mass of the Earth's surface. Some are just a few million years old. Others formed almost 4 billion years ago, when the Earth was young but they are always being added to as new rock forms. Rocks come in many shapes, colours and textures, but all form in three main ways: igneous (forms from cooled magma), sedimentary (forms in layers on the seabed) or metamorphic rock (changed rock). As magma cools, gems often form in gas bubbles, called geodes. Some gems with a high melting point form directly from magma, such as diamonds and rubies.

Rock is broken down by weather

Lava cools to form igneous rock

Rock fragments are washed down into the sea

Rock debris settles on the seabed forming new sedimentary rock

▲ Rocks are continually broken down and then remade in the rock cycle.

Hot magma erupts through volcanoes

►► **Read further › folding rock**
pg21 (b28)

Rock cycle
The materials from which rocks are made are continually recycled to make new rocks. This process is called the rock cycle. Hot magma, the molten rock from Earth's interior *(see pg22 [w11])*, cools to form igneous rock that is gradually broken down by the weather. The fragments are washed down in rivers to the sea where they settle on the seabed *(see pg30 [p9])* forming layers of sedimentary rock. Both igneous and sedimentary rocks may change into metamorphic rock when they are crushed by earthquakes or cooked by volcanoes.

►► **Read further › elements**
pg9 (c28)

Rock grains
All rocks are made of tiny crystals or grains of naturally occurring chemicals called minerals. Some rocks are made from just one mineral; others contain six or more. There are more than 2000 different kinds of mineral, but only 30 or so occur commonly. The most common are the silicates, such as quartz, made from a combination of chemicals including oxygen and silicon.

Gypsum

Barite

Calcite

Quartz

Galena

Pyrite

◄ Minerals include common substances such as rock salt and rare ones such as gold and gems.

Eighty per cent of all volcanic rocks are basalt

IT'S A FACT

• The rarest gems are called precious gems and include diamonds, emeralds and rubies.

• The acid in rain can dissolve limestone rock, leaving behind caves and potholes.

▸ *Constant baking in desert heat can make layers of rock flake off.*

▾ *Rocks may even be shattered by spreading tree roots as they grow.*

Rock breaking

Rock may be tough, but exposure to weather eventually breaks even the hardest rock into soft sand and clay. The weather attacks rock with moisture, heat and cold, and acid chemicals in rainwater. The more extreme the climate, the faster rock weathers. Typically, rocks on the surface are the most affected, but water trickling down through the ground can attack the rock beneath as well.

▸▸ **Read further › extreme climate pg35 (b22)**

▸ *Frost getting into cracks high in mountains can shatter rocks.*

DOWN TO EARTH

• When water freezes in cracks in rocks, it expands and splits the rock with an estimated force of 3000 kg on an area the size of a postage stamp.

• Some rocks, such as chalk, are made almost completely from the remains of sea creatures.

 Check it out!

• http://rocksforkids.com
• http://www.surfnetkids.com/rocks.htm

a
b
c
d
e
f
g
h
i
j
k
l
m
n
o
p
q
r
s
t
u
v
w

Mountain high

MOUNTAINS LOOK solid and unchanging, but they are being built up, then worn away by the weather, all the time. The world's highest mountains were actually formed quite recently in the Earth's history. The Himalayas, for instance, were built up in the last 40 million years, and are still growing, even today. The most ancient mountain ranges have long been worn flat, or reduced to hills, such as New York's Adirondacks, which are now over 1 billion years old.

Neat folds

A few mountains, such as Washington's Mount St Helens, are volcanoes – tall cones built up by successive eruptions of lava and ash. Most, however, are thrown up by the immense power of the Earth's crust moving. Some are huge slabs called fault blocks, or 'horst', caused by powerful earthquakes. But all the world's great mountain ranges, such as the Andes and Rockies, were made by the crumpling of rock layers as tectonic plates pushed against each other. Such mountains are called fold mountains.

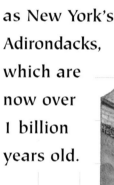

▸ *Three types of mountain range.*

Volcanic peak

Fold mountain

Fault block mountain

▶▶ **Read further › formation of volcanoes**
pg23 (b22)

To scale
Each square = 1000 m

The highest mountains – measured from sea level to summit – in each continent, to scale

Jayakusuma (Oceania)	Elbrus (Europe)	Kilimanjaro (Africa)	McKinley (North America)	Aconcagua (South America)	Everest (Asia)
5030 m	5642 m	5895 m	6194 m	6960 m	8863 m

Mount Everest is growing slightly taller every year by a few millimetres

1 2 3 4 5 6 7 8 9 10 11 12 13 14 15 16 17 18 19

a
b
c
d
e
f
g
h
i
j
k
l
m
n
o
p
q
r
s
t
u
v
w

IT'S A FACT

• If you travelled from London to Paris and back again eight times, you would cover the same distance as the length of the Andes mountain range.

• The largest recorded volcanic eruption happened in 1550 BC in Santorini, Greece.

Folding rock

Read further > folds
pg20 (b14)

Most rocks form in flat layers called strata. Some rocks are sedimentary and form from sand and mud settling on the seabed. Others are volcanic, such as the vast basalt plateaux at the heart of many continents. Fold mountains build up where the movement of the Earth's crust tilts, crumples and squeezes, and lifts these flat layers.

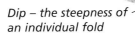

Strike – the direction of the folding movement

Dip – the steepness of an individual fold

The Himalayas

Himalayan mountains

The Himalayas were thrown up by the collision between India and the rest of Asia. India has been ploughing relentlessly north into Asia for the last 40 million years. As it does so, layer upon layer of rock in Asia's southern edge has crumpled, like the bow wave of a boat pushing through water or sludgy mud. While India carries on moving, the Himalayas will continue to crumple up in front of it.

Asian plate

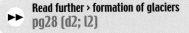
Folded rock layers

India moving north

Read further > faults
pg25 (b22)

Read further > formation of glaciers
pg28 (d2; l2)

Round the block

As the Earth's crust moves during earthquakes (*see pg24 [m13]*), huge blocks of rock can slip or 'fault'. Sometimes, they move just a few millimetres. Occasionally, they move over many metres. But over millions of years, successive movements can move a block up or down huge distances. In California's Sierra Nevada, faulting has created a steep slope 3350 m high and hundreds of kilometres long.

▸ *Geologists describe fault movements using these terms.*

▲ *All 14 of the world's peaks over 8000 m are in the Himalayas – in Nepal, China and Kashmir.*

Throw

Heave

Fault plane – the surface of the slipping block

WORLD'S HIGHEST

Mountains	Height
Everest	8863 m
K2	8610 m
Kanchenjunga	8598 m
Lhotse	8511 m
Makalu	8481 m

The tallest mountain on Earth – Mauna Kea in Hawaii – stands 10,200 m tall when measured from ocean floor to summit

Fiery mountains

VOLCANOES ARE places where hot molten rock or magma wells up to the surface from deep within the Earth's interior. Sometimes, the magma flows out over the ground as red-hot liquid rock or lava. At other times, the volcano becomes clogged up with a thick plug of magma, then suddenly erupts in a gigantic explosion that sends up jets of steam and hurls fiery fragments of magma high into the air. Successive eruptions can build up such a huge cone of ash and lava around the volcano that it becomes a mountain (see pg20 [i8]).

DOWN TO EARTH

• The eruption of Mount Tambora in Java in 1815 sent up so much ash that the Sun was blocked throughout the world, giving two years of cool, wet summers.

• One of the most gigantic eruptions in history occurred in Yellowstone, in the USA, 2.2 million years ago. It poured out enough magma to build today's biggest volcano six times over.

IT'S A FACT

• The biggest recent eruption in the USA was from Mount St Helens in 1980.

• The eruption of the volcanic island of Krakatoa near Java in 1883 could be heard a quarter of the way around the world!

All fired up

The biggest volcanic eruptions are powered by a combination of steam and carbon dioxide gas. They remain dissolved in the magma inside the volcano because of the extreme pressure. But as the plug of magma breaks, the pressure is suddenly released, creating an explosion big enough to send chunks of rock the size of houses many thousands of metres up into the air.

Eruptions begin with a build-up of pressure in the magma chamber beneath the volcano

As the steam and gas jet out, they carry with them clouds of ash and larger fragments of the broken plug of magma, called volcanic bombs or tephra

Bubbles of steam and gas form and swell rapidly inside the magma, and burst out like the froth from a violently shaken bottle of fizz

With the volcanic plug out of the way, magma surges up and out of the volcano, and flows down as lava

◄ *Magma chamber inside a volcano.*

There are around 1500 active volcanoes around the world

1   2   3   4   5   6   7   8   9   10   11   12   13   14   15   16   17   18   19

a
b
c
d
e
f
g
h
i
j
k
l
m
n
o
p
q
r
s
t
u
v
w

Types of volcano

►► **Read further > tectonic plates**
pg17 (b22); pg25 (b22)

Most volcanoes occur near cracks between the giant tectonic plates that make up the Earth's surface, but they come in many different shapes and sizes. Spectacular, violently erupting volcanic cones, or 'cone' volcanoes, develop where the plates are pushing together *(see pg17 [q26])*. Here, magma is trapped below ground, making it so acidic – and so thick and sticky – that it clogs up the volcano and then erupts sporadically and dramatically. Where plates are pulling apart, the magma is less acid and runnier. It reaches the surface easily and floods out steadily as lava to form a gentle slope that looks like an upturned shield, known as a 'shield' volcano.

Cone volcano   *Shield volcano*

▸ *Volcanoes in the Pacific spray out fiery lava fountains.*

Rock soup

The lava that gushes from the Hawaiian volcanoes in the Pacific is very runny. Because of this, the explosive gases leak out, and so the lava rarely bursts out in a huge explosion. Instead, it tends to spray out frequently in fiery fountains, or well out in slower streams of molten rock.

►► **Read further > volcanic eruptions**
pg22 (n2)

Boiling fountains

Even if magma does not erupt in a volcano, its tremendous heat can produce other effects. Rainwater trickling into the ground, for instance, may be heated under pressure, then burst on to the surface in a tremendous whoosh of steam called a geyser. Or a mix of hot water and mud may bubble up on the surface to create baths of boiling mud called mudpots. Sometimes, hot fumes of toxic gases escape through cracks in the rock to emerge like smoke from a chimney in 'fumaroles'.

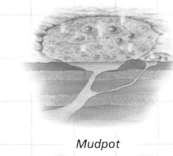

Mudpot

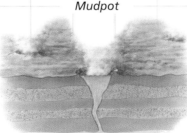

Fumarole

▾ *Geyser blowing superheated steam.*

►► **Read further > black smokers**
pg31 (l31)

Top notch

When a volcano erupts, it can completely empty the magma chamber as lava, ash and other debris are blown out. This leaves the top of the cone unsupported, and it collapses into the volcanic vent. This creates a huge pit or crater in the summit of the volcano. Once the volcano stops erupting, the crater may gradually fill with water to form a lake, such as Oregon's famous Crater Lake.

🌐 **Check it out!**

- http://volcano.und.nodak.edu/vwdocs/kids/kids.html
- http://www.fema.gov/kids/volcano.htm

►► **Read further > lakes**
p27 (c34)

After three years of forming, an island called Surtsey, near Iceland appeared ten days after a volcanic eruption in 1963

Shaky ground

THE GROUND sometimes trembles when a heavy truck passes by. But major earthquakes that make the ground shudder violently are set off by the movement of tectonic plates – the giant slabs of rock that make up the Earth's surface *(see pg17 [c34])*. Tectonic plates are moving all the time, radiating minor tremors as they grind past each other. But every now and then they get jammed. Then the pressure builds up until they suddenly lurch on again, sending out vibrations, called shock waves, in all directions and creating major earthquakes that can bring down mountains and destroy cities.

(see pg17 [c34])

IT'S A FACT

• The world's most deadly earthquake occurred in Shanxi in China in 1556, killing about 830,000 people.

• In 1995, an earthquake struck Kobe in Japan, killing 5200 people, destroying more than 100,000 buildings and leaving about 250,000 people homeless.

▾ *Earthquakes start where slabs of the Earth's surface are moving in opposite directions.*

Epicentre

Hypocentre (focus)

Radiating shock waves

Shock waves

In an earthquake, shock waves radiate out in circles from its origin or hypocentre (focus). Shock waves vibrate throughout the ground, but it is at the surface that they do most damage. Damage is most severe at the epicentre – the point on the surface directly above the focus – where the shock waves are strongest. But they can often be felt up to thousands of kilometres away.

Check it out!

• http://www.fema.gov/kids/quake.htm
• http://earthquake.usgs.gov/4kids/
• http://www.yahooligans.com/Science_and
   _Nature/The_Earth/Geology/Plat_
   Tectonics/earthquakes/

▲ *Devastation to buildings caused by a Taiwanese earthquake in 1999.*

DOWN TO EARTH

• Most earthquakes last less than a minute. The longest recorded, in Alaska on 21 March 1964, lasted four minutes.

• Typically, tectonic plates slide only 4 or 5 cm past each other each year. In a slip that triggers a major earthquake, they can move 1 metre or more.

• In most earthquakes a few minor tremors (foreshocks) are followed by an intense burst lasting 1 or 2 minutes.

During the 1989 San Francisco earthquake, a crack 650 m wide opened up in the Santa Cruz mountains

Earthquake zones

Places near the edges of tectonic plates, such as south-east Europe and the Pacific coast, are at a very high risk of earthquakes. In these earthquake zones, minor quakes are frequent, and a quiet period may often be the build-up to a really big one. People in California, USA, are constantly threatened by the movement of the San Andreas fault, where two great tectonic plates grind past each other *(see pg17 [c34])*. When the San Andreas fault juddered in 1906, it set off earthquakes that destroyed San Francisco.

▶▶ **Read further › earthquake devastation**
pg24 (m2)

▼ *Earthquakes and volcanoes occur in the same regions, where tectonic plates meet.*

Measuring earthquakes

Seismologists (scientists who study earthquakes) measure the strength of the shock waves with a device called a seismometer. They then grade the severity of the quake on the Richter scale, from 1 (slight tremor) to over 9 (devastating quake). The Richter scale shows the size of an earthquake – its absolute magnitude – but not its effects. So experts also rate an earthquake on the Mercalli scale, which assesses the damage on a scale of 1 (barely noticeable) to 12 (total destruction), expressed in Roman numerals, I to XII.

A seismometer records earthquake vibrations as up and down lines on paper or displays them on a computer screen

MERCALLI SCALE

III – light fittings shake

VI – windows shatter

VIII – chimneys shaken down

X – major structural damage to bridges

Tidal waves

The world's most awesome waves are called tidal waves or tsunami (pronounced 'soon-army') which are caused by earthquakes (see *pg24 [t10]*). Undersea earthquakes or a landslide into the sea can send out a giant pulse of water racing along the seabed as fast as a jet plane. When the pulse reaches shallow water, a huge wave tens of metres high rears up, swamping anything in its path.

As the pulse moves into shallow water it rears into a giant wave and swamps coastal regions

A shift in the seabed sends out a pulse of water

▶▶ **Read further › tectonic plates**
pg21 (o22)

In 1958, the biggest-ever recorded tsunami occurred in Alaska, measuring 524 m high and travelling at 160 km/h

a b c d e f g h i j k l m n o p q r s t u v w

Water on the land

THE AMOUNT of water in the world remains constant, but is continually moving around the Earth and its atmosphere in a process called the water cycle. Rain falling from clouds gathers in rivers, lakes and oceans. Heat from the Sun causes the water to evaporate (become water vapour). As the water vapour rises into the atmosphere, it cools and condenses (changes back into water) and forms clouds. When the water in the clouds becomes too heavy, it falls back to Earth as rain and returns to the rivers. Some of the rain soaks into the ground and is used by plants. Plants return unused water as it evaporates from their leaves (transpiration).

Water, water everywhere

There is a huge amount of water in the world – over 525 million cubic km – but 97 per cent is salt water in the sea. The other 3 per cent is fresh water, but most of this is frozen in ice sheets at the poles, or deep underground. Only a very tiny portion moves round in the water cycle, but this precious water keeps rivers flowing and provides us with water to drink and plants with the water they need for growth.

1. *Water evaporates from the sea and lakes and the water vapour rises into the air*

2. *Water is taken up from the ground by plants and transpires from their leaves*

3. *As the water vapour rises, it cools and condenses into droplets of water and ice crystals to form clouds*

4. *When the water is too heavy to be held by the clouds, they drop their moisture as rain*

5. *Falling rain gathers into rivers and runs directly down to the sea, or seeps into the ground, where it may be taken up by plants*

To scale

Each square = 1000 km

The longest rivers in each continent. *The Amazon and the Nile can be measured from various points, thus their official lengths sometimes change*

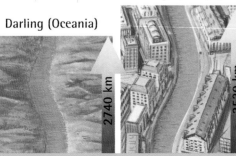
Darling (Oceania)
2740 km

Volga (Europe)
3530 km

Mississippi-Missouri (North America)
6020 km

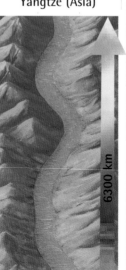
Yangtze (Asia)
6300 km

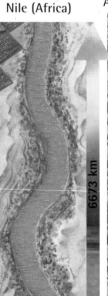
Nile (Africa)
6673 km

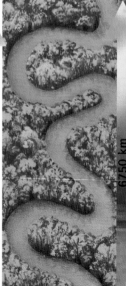
Amazon (South America)
6750 km

The Mississippi flushes 17,584 cubic metres of water into the Gulf of Mexico every second

1   2   3   4   5   6   7   8   9   10   11   12   13   14   15   16   17   18   19

▶▶ **Read further › lakes**
pg23 (k34)

IT'S A FACT

• The world's shortest recorded river is the North Fork Foe River in Montana, USA, at 17.7 m long.

• Lake Superior is the largest freshwater lake in the world, bigger than Ireland. It is 560 km long, with a surface area of 82,100 sq km.

Lake Superior
Lake Michigan
Lake Huron
Lake Ontario
Lake Erie

Great lakes

Many of the largest lakes in North America and Europe were created barely 10,000 years ago, during the last ice age. Lakes of water melting from the ice-filled hollows were gouged out both by the glaciers themselves *(see pg28 [u9])* and by the huge floods of water released when the glaciers melted. The Great Lakes were probably created this way, including Lake Superior.

Rivers run down

Whenever there is enough rain or melting snow to keep them flowing, rivers run down to the sea or to lakes. In wetter parts of the world, they are kept flowing even when it is not raining or snowing, from water underground. In fact, a lot of rain does not flow straight over the land, but seeps into the ground, then bubbles out again lower down in places called springs.

▸ *Lake Miramar in Argentina.*

▶▶ **Read further › seas and oceans**
pg30 (d2)

Deltas

A river slows down as it flows into the sea, so it can no longer carry the load of silt it has collected along the way. Often, the silt is dumped in a fan-shape, or a delta, and the river splits into branches called distributaries. Where there is a strong coastal current, the head of the delta is swept into a curving or 'arcuate' form such as the Nile in Africa. Where the sea current is weak, the distributaries spread out in a ragged 'bird's foot' shape such as the Mississippi delta.

Most rivers start as tiny brooks high in the hills, tumbling over rocks and rapids

As they flow on down, brooks grow into big streams as they are joined by other streams called tributaries

Further down, streams broaden into rivers that flow through deep, meandering (winding) channels of sediment, washed down from higher up

◂ *An arcuate delta.*

DOWN TO EARTH

• Oxbow lakes form when a river meanders (changes course) cutting off patches of water before linking back up (braiding).

• Lake Baikal in Russia is the world's deepest lake. At 1743 m, it holds 20 per cent of the world's fresh water.

Check it out!

• http://www.amrivers.org/kids/riverstory.htm

• http://www.geography4kids.com/files/water_hydrosphere.html

The highest waterfall on Earth is the 979 m-high Angel Falls in Venezuela

a b c d e f g h i j k l m n o p q r s t u v w

Rivers of ice

- The longest glacier in the world is the Lambert–Fisher Ice Passage in Antarctica, at 515 km long. North America's Hubbard Glacier is 158 km long.

- In an ice age, the weather alternates between cold spells, called glacials, and warm spells, called interglacials. The last ice age, which began 2 million years ago, had 17 glacials – the most recent of which ended only 10,000 years ago.

IT CAN BE so cold in high mountain regions that snow never melts. It builds up over many years, compacting into a mass of ice. Eventually, the ice may become so heavy that it starts to flow very slowly downhill, forming rivers of ice called glaciers as it funnels into valleys. Nowadays, glaciers only form in the highest mountains and in polar regions. But in the past, in cold periods called ice ages, glaciers were far more widespread. Huge areas of North America and Europe were under ice, which left dramatic marks on the landscape.

1. The ice in glaciers is not clear, but opaque like dirty snowballs, and dirty with grit

Slow movers

Glaciers move very, very slowly, but their sheer weight gives them enormous power to carve out the landscape. They gouge out huge, U-shaped valleys, scoop deep hollows called cirques, and truncate (slice away) entire hills. Glaciers also move huge amounts of rock debris, shattered from the mountains by frost, and deposit it in massive piles called moraines.

▼ The dense ice in glaciers is made from thousands of years of snow. As new snow falls, the old snow beneath it is squeezed in a process called firnification.

2. Cracks or crevasses appear in the ice where the glacier bends over bumps in the valley floor

3. The ice is striped with moraine (rock debris) fallen from the mountain slopes above

4. The glacier melts lower down where the air is warmer

Check it out!

- http://www.surfnetkids.com/glacier.htm
- http://www.athropolis.com/links/iceberg.htm
- http://www.glacier.rice/edu

If all the ice in Antarctica melted, the world's oceans would rise by 60 to 70 metres

1 2 3 4 5 6 7 8 9 10 11 12 13 14 15 16 17 18 19

a b c d e f g h i j k l m n o p q r s t u v w

▸ *Around 15,000 icebergs calve each year in the Arctic.*

Floating ice

Icebergs are huge chunks of ice that break off at the edge of glaciers (polar ice) and float out to sea. Ice that breaks off is called calving. This often happens when tides or waves wobble the ice sheet up and down, especially in summer when the ice is weaker. In the Arctic, icebergs vary from truck-sized bergs called growlers to huge ones the size of an apartment block.

Read further › tidal bulge
pg31 (b33)

IT'S A FACT

• The biggest ever Antarctic iceberg was 300 km long, spotted in 1956 by the USS *Glacier*.

• Seven-eighths of an iceberg is submerged under the sea.

Snow business

Outside the tropics, most rain begins to fall from clouds as snow because it is cold high up. The snow usually melts to rain as it falls into warmer air, but if the air is cold enough, the snow will flutter all the way to the ground without melting. Snowflakes are made of masses of tiny crystals. These crystals grow together in an infinite variety of shapes and no one has ever found an identical pair.

▾ *Snowflakes are always six-sided.*

Read further › ice crystals
pg33 (f30)

Antarctica

Antarctica is the coldest, driest, windiest continent on Earth. Even in summer, temperatures rarely climb over −25°C and the thermometer at the Vostok science station has shown −89.2°C. For the past 5 million years, 98 per cent of Antarctica has been covered in ice almost 5 km deep in places. Locked up in all this ice is 70 per cent of the world's freshwater *(see pg27 [g30])*.

Read further › wind
pg33 (m30)

▴ *The bleak landscape of Antarctica, measuring 14 million square km, is uninhabited and used only for scientific research.*

Washington and London were buried under 1.5 km of ice 18,000 years ago

22 23 24 25 26 27 28 29 30 31 32 33 34 35 36 37 38 39

Ocean deep

THERE ARE five great oceans: the Pacific, the Atlantic, the Indian, the Arctic, and the Southern Ocean around Antarctica. There are also many seas, including the Mediterranean and the Red Sea. Until recently, we knew little more about the bottom of the oceans than we did about the surface of Mars. Now, surveys undertaken with sound equipment and computerized underwater craft have revealed a hugely varied landscape on the ocean bed, with high mountains, wide plains and deep valleys.

● IT'S A FACT

• The West Wind Drift (an ocean current) around Antarctica moves 2000 times as much water as the Amazon does each year.

• Oceans are, on average, about 2000 m deep.

• One of the tides in the Pacific Ocean reaches 9 m inland, along the coast of Korea.

● Into the abyss

Around the edge of the ocean is a shelf of shallow water called the continental shelf. At the edge of the shelf, the ocean bed plunges steeply to the deep ocean floor, known as the 'abyssal plain'. This plain is vast, but not completely flat. In the Pacific especially, it is dotted with huge mountains, called seamounts. The world's longest mountain chain, the mid-ocean ridge, runs down through the Atlantic and into the Indian Ocean.

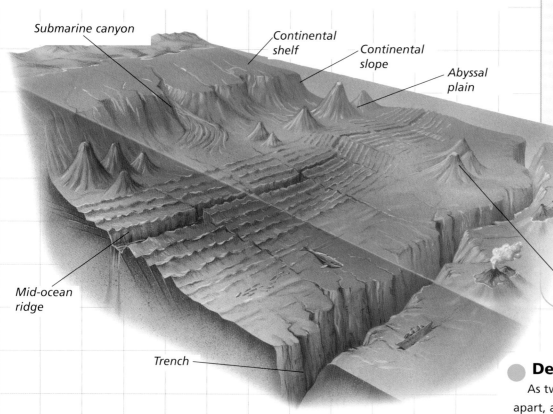

Submarine canyon

Continental shelf

Continental slope

Abyssal plain

Mid-ocean ridge

Trench

Seamount

🌐 Check it out!

• http://podaac.jpl.nasa.gov/kids/
• http://science.whoi.edu/Dive Discover/
• http://www.pbs.org/wgbh/nova/abyss/

▸ *The bathyscaphe called Trieste that visited the ocean floor in 1961.*

● Deep dive

As two giant tectonic plates move apart, a deep gash opens up in the ocean floor – an ocean trench. The deepest point on the Earth's surface is the Challenger Deep in the Marianas Trench in the west Pacific, 10,920 m deep. In 1960, the *Trieste*, an underwater craft or bathyscaphe, dived almost to the bottom.

At the deepest point in the ocean, water pressure is 8 tonnes per square centimetre

1   2   3   4   5   6   7   8   9   10   11   12   13   14   15   16   17   18   19

One high tide bulge occurs at places in the ocean nearest to the Moon, as water is pulled towards the Moon

Another high tide bulge occurs in places furthest from the Moon, because the solid Earth, too, is pulled towards the Moon, leaving the ocean waters behind

The sea moves or 'flows' upwards and inland as the tide rises

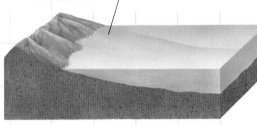

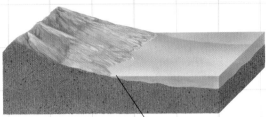

The sea ebbs, sinking and retreating, as the tide drops

Rising and falling

All around the world, the sea rises and falls slightly twice every day in 'tides'. As the sea rises, it flows further up seashores. As it falls back, it slowly retreats or 'ebbs'. Tides are caused by the pull of the Moon's gravity on the oceans' waters as the Earth spins around. High tides move around the Earth in two bulges on opposite sides of the Earth. Spring tides (high tides) happen twice a month. They occur as the Moon and Sun line up with each other, combining their gravitational pull.

▶▶ **Read further › spinning Earth**
pg10 (d2)

DOWN TO EARTH

• The most extreme spring tides are in the Bay of Fundy in Canada, where the sea rises and falls up to 15 m.

• The Dead Sea is the lowest sea on Earth, at 400 m below sea level.

▶▶ **Read further › geysers**
pg23 (l22)

Undersea chimneys

In deep valleys in the mid-ocean ridges, there are amazing natural chimneys on the seabed. Called black smokers or hydrothermal vents, these chimneys are volcanic features *(see pg23 [q30])* that billow black fumes of hot gases and water. Seawater seeping into cracks in the seafloor is heated by hot volcanic magma *(see pg22 [w11])*. The heated water dissolves minerals from seabed rock and spews from the vents in scalding, mineral-rich black plumes.

▸ *Plumes from black smokers.*

Calm waters

The Pacific is the world's largest ocean. It is twice as large as the Atlantic and covers an area of 181 million sq km – one-third of the world. The Pacific is peppered with thousands of islands – many are the peaks of undersea volcanoes and most are only about 1 m above sea level. The word 'pacific' means calm.

▾ *On average, the Pacific Ocean is 4200 m deep.*

▶▶ **Read further › undersea volcanoes**
pg31 (l31)

If all the salt was removed from the oceans, it would cover the continents to a depth of 1 metre

Swirling air

THE ATMOSPHERE that surrounds the Earth is barely thicker on the Earth than the peel is on an orange. Yet without it, the Earth would be as lifeless as the Moon. The atmosphere absorbs the Sun's warmth, yet shields the Earth from its most harmful rays. It gives us clean, fresh water to drink (*see pg26 [j11]*), and provides us with the air that we, and most other animals, need to breathe. Our weather is also a result of changes in the Earth's atmosphere. These changes are caused by worldwide and local variations in the heat of the Sun.

DOWN TO EARTH

• The impact of particles from the Sun on the gases of the upper atmosphere creates shimmering curtains of light called auroras in the night sky over polar regions.

• The atmosphere is a mixture of gases: 78 per cent nitrogen, 21 per cent oxygen and 1 per cent argon and carbon dioxide, plus traces of neon, krypton, zenon, helium, nitrous oxide and methane.

Atmospheric layers

The atmosphere may look invisible but it has a number of distinct layers or 'spheres'. At the bottom is the troposphere – only 10 km thick, but containing over 70 per cent of the atmosphere's gases by weight. Above that, the gases become thinner and thinner with each layer, until at about 800 km up, they are so thin or 'rarified' that it is hard to tell where the atmosphere ends and where empty space begins.

IT'S A FACT

• The world's windiest place is George V island in Antarctica, where winds often blow at 320 km/h.

• Temperatures drop to nearly –60°C at the top of the troposphere.

Check it out!
• http://www.enchantedlearning.com/subjects/ astronomy/planets/earth/Atmosphere.shtml
• http://www.windpower.org/en/kids/choose/wind/ tropos.htm

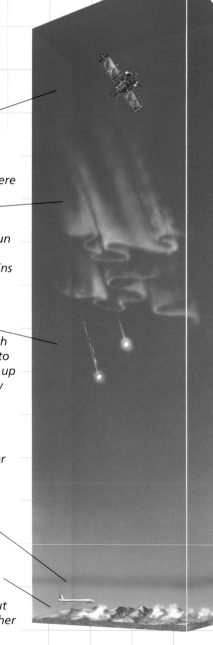

Exosphere:
500–800 km
Contains hardly any gas; low-level satellites orbit here

Thermosphere:
80–500 km
Becomes roasted by the Sun to up to 1800°C, but is so thin in gases that it contains little real heat

Mesosphere:
50–80 km
Is too thin to soak up much heat, but is thick enough to stop meteorites that burn up leaving fiery trails in the sky

Stratosphere:
10–50 km
Contains the ozone layer and becomes hotter higher up; little water and no weather; airliners cruise here in the still air

Troposphere:
0–10 km
Contains three-quarters of the atmosphere's gases and nearly all its water; temperatures drop by about 6.5°C every kilometre further

Cirrus

Cumulonimbus

Cirrostratus

Nimbostratus

Stratus

Cumulus

▲ *The main classes of cloud were named in the 1800s by Luke Howard, a British weather scientist.*

Clouds

Clouds are made of tiny drops of water *(see pg26 [h13])* and ice crystals *(see pg29 [k35])* so light they float in the air. There is a large variety of clouds, but only two main shapes: fluffy, heaped 'cumulus' that form clouds when air moisture billows upwards; and flat 'stratus' clouds that form when a layer of air cools down enough for its water content to condense. Both types of cloud take different forms at different heights in the sky.

▶▶ **Read further › ice crystals**
pg29 (b34)

▶▶ **Read further › global warming / air pressure**
pg13 (c31); pg35 (o22)

Hot and cold

Winds blow because the Sun warms some places more than others, creating differences in air pressure (density) that push air about. In warm places, air expands and rises, lowering the pressure. In cool spots, the air is heavy and sinks, raising the pressure. Winds blow from zones where pressure is high, called anticyclones, to zones where it is low, called cyclones or depressions. The bigger the difference in pressure, the stronger the wind.

▶▶ **Read further › twisters / hurricanes**
pg34 (m2); pg35 (b22)

World winds

Winds often blow from the same, or prevailing, direction in each of three belts around the world. In polar regions, cool, sinking air drives the prevailing winds away from the poles. In the tropics, warm air rising over the Equator draws winds in from either side. In the mid-latitudes in between, winds are driven away from the tropics by cool air sinking. Yet none of these winds blows directly north to south, because the world is spinning. So winds veer off to the left in the southern hemisphere and the right in the northern hemisphere.

▼ *Northern hemisphere.* ▼ *Southern hemisphere.*

Winds spiral clockwise from high pressure zones and anticlockwise into low pressure zones.

Winds spiral in the opposite direction

Tropics – dry trade winds blow from the south-east or north-east towards the Equator, depending on the time of year

Mid-latitudes – warm, moist, westerly winds (winds from the west) are common

Polar regions – cold, easterly winds blow for much of the year

Cumulonimbus (thunder) clouds in the tropics can increase in size to reach a height of 20 km

a b c d e f g h i j k l m n o p q r s t u v w

Stormy Weather

W HEN STORMS rage, winds blow hard and rains pour down from thick grey clouds. Some storms, such as summer thunderstorms, are over in a few minutes, while tropical hurricanes can blow for over a day. But all storms share the same cause – a powerful combination of heat and lots of moisture. Summer thunderstorms happen when the hot morning sun steams water off the ground to pile up into towering thunderclouds that unleash torrents of rain. Hurricanes occur when these huge thunderclouds mushroom over warm oceans and join together into one giant, spiralling storm system.

Twister

Tornadoes occur when a funnel of violently spinning air forms beneath a thundercloud and swoops to the ground. At the centre is an area of low pressure that sucks up everything in its path like a giant vacuum cleaner, while the terrifying winds can race around at speeds of over 400 km/h, tossing people, cars and buildings in the air like toys. From March to July every year, about 700 of these storms whirl across the Midwest of America in an area known as Tornado Alley.

▶▶ Read further > winds
pg33 (m30)

◀ Tornado Alley in the US Midwest, where tornadoes are also known as twisters.

Electric sky

Thunderclouds are built up by strong updrafts on warm, humid days, or along a cold front. These clouds are so big that raindrops grow to huge sizes within them. Whirlwinds within the clouds hurl the drops together so violently that the clouds become charged with static electricity. Eventually, the charge is released in a massive flash of lightning.

▶ A thundercloud unleashes forks of lightning.

A flash of lightning is brighter than 10 million ordinary light bulbs

1   2   3   4   5   6   7   8   9   10   11   12   13   14   15   16   17   18   19

Hurricane force

Hurricanes are huge tropical storms that develop over the eastern Atlantic Ocean, then wheel westwards towards the east coast of the Americas. By this time, the storm is spiralling around a tight centre or 'eye' around which rains pour and winds gust at up to 320 km/h. Each hurricane is given a name and tracked by satellite to give people plenty of warning that one is on its way – but when it arrives, dragging with it a huge surge of seawater *(see pg25 [q38])*, the impact is devastating.

▶▶ **Read further › weathering**
   pg19 [h30]

▸ *Satellite view showing the eye of a hurricane.*

WORLD'S WORST

Worst weather	Disaster
• Most thunder	Tororo, Uganda, Africa averages 250 thundery days a year
• Worst hailstorm	a hailstorm in 1888 battered to death 246 people in India
• Worst hurricane	Hurricane Flora in 1963 killed 6000 people in the Caribbean

IT'S A FACT

• Hurricanes can be 800 km across, and take 18 hours or more to pass.

• There are about 45 hurricanes every year.

Frontal storms

Between the tropics and polar regions, in most of North America, the stormiest weather is often linked to moving depressions (low pressure zones). Depressions are mostly cold air, but a wedge of warm air intrudes into them and the worst weather occurs along the boundaries of this wedge, called fronts, where the warm air meets the cold air. As a depression moves past, these fronts bring a distinct sequence of weather.

First to arrive is the warm front, where warm air rides up gently over the cold air, bringing steady rain over long periods

After the warm front passes, there is a brief respite, then the cold front arrives. Here the cold air sharply undercuts the warm air, piling up thunderclouds and unleashing short, but heavy, rain showers and stirring up winds

▶▶ **Read further › air pressure**
   pg33 [j22]

A single thunderstorm generates the energy of a hydrogen bomb

Glossary

Abyssal plain The broad plain on the deep seabed, 5000 m down and covered in ooze.

Acid rain All rain is slightly acidic, but acid rain forms when pollution by sulphur dioxide and nitrogen reacts in sunlight with oxygen and moisture in the air.

Atmosphere The thick layer of gases surrounding the Earth.

Aurora Spectacular displays of coloured lights in the night sky above the North and South poles.

Biome A complete community of plants, animals and other living things existing in similar conditions over a large region, such as tropical rainforests or the prairies.

Black smoker Small volcanic chimneys on the seabed that throw out black fumes of superheated water.

Continental crust The ancient, thick part of the Earth's crust under the continents.

Continental drift The process whereby continents move slowly around the world.

Core The dense, hot centre of the Earth.

Crust The solid outer shell of the Earth, varying from 5 to 80 km thick.

Delta A flat piece of land, which has built up from material such as silt that has been deposited by a river as it flows to the sea.

Earthquake A brief, violent shaking of the Earth's surface, typically set off by the movement of tectonic plates.

Ecosystem A local community of plants, animals and other living things interacting with their surroundings.

Era, geological One of the three major divisions of the last 500 million years of Earth's history: the Palaeozoic, the Mesozoic and the Cenozoic.

Exosphere The layer of the atmosphere above the thermosphere, beginning 500 km up.

Fault A fracture in rock where one block of rock slides past another.

Fossil the preserved remains of a creature or plant long dead, usually turned to stone.

Front The boundary between where a warm or wet mass of air meets a cold or dry mass of air in the atmosphere.

Glaciation The moulding of the landscape by glaciers and ice sheets.

Greenhouse effect The way certain gases in the atmosphere trap the Sun's heat like the panes of glass in a greenhouse.

Ice age A long cold period when huge areas of the Earth are covered by ice sheets.

Igneous rock Rocks created as hot magma from the Earth's interior cool and solidify.

Lava Hot molten rock emerging through volcanoes, known as magma when underground.

Lithosphere The rigid outer shell of the Earth, including the crust and the rigid upper part of the mantle.

Magma Hot molten rock in the Earth's interior. It is known as lava when it emerges to the surface of the Earth.

Mantle The warm layer of the Earth's interior below the crust. Every now and then parts of the upper mantle melt to form magma.

Mesosphere The layer of the atmosphere above the stratosphere, beginning 50 km up.

Metamorphic rock Rocks created by the alteration of other rocks by heat or pressure.

Meteorite A rock from space that crashes into the Earth's surface.

Mid-ocean ridge A ridge down the middle of the sea floor where tectonic plates meet.

Moraine Sand and gravel deposited in piles by a glacier or ice sheet.

Ozone hole A large region over the Arctic where the ozone layer is very sparse.

Ozone layer A layer of ozone (a form of oxygen gas) high in the stratosphere that protects us from the Sun's radiation.

Period, geological One of the major periods of time into which the Earth's history is divided, each lasting many millions of years.

Planetesimal One of the small lumps of rock circling the early Sun which later clumped together to form the planets.

Rift valley A valley formed when land drops between two faults, typically as a continent begins to split.

Sea mount A mountain under the sea.

Strata Layers of sedimentary rock.

Stratosphere The layer of atmosphere above the troposphere, beginning 10 km up, where temperatures rise with height.

Subduction The bending of a tectonic plate beneath another as they collide.

Tectonic plate The 20 or so giant slabs of rock that make up the Earth's surface.

Tor An outcrop of bare, weathered rock on a smooth hilltop.

Thermosphere The layer of the atmosphere above the mesosphere, beginning 80 km up.

Troposphere The lowest layer of the atmosphere existing up to 10 km.

Weathering The breakdown of rock when exposed to the weather.

Index

Entries in bold refer to main subjects; entries in italics refer to illustrations.

A

abyssal plain 30, *30*
acid rain 13, 19
Aconcagua, Mount 20, *20*
Adirondacks 20
Africa 8, 16, 19
air *see* atmosphere
air pressure 33
Alaska 17, 24, 25
altostratus clouds 33
aluminium 9
Amazon, River 26, *26*, 27, 30
ammonia 14
Andes, Mountains 20, 21
Angel Falls 27
Antarctica 8, *29*, 30
  climate 12, 29
  continental drift 16, 17
  glaciers 28
  ice 29
  winds 32
anticyclones 33
aphelion 11
Arctic 17, 29
Arctic Ocean 30
argon 32
Asia 8, 16, 21, 35
Atlantic Ocean 16, 17, 30, 35
atmosphere 8, **32–33**, *32*
  oxygen 15
  pollution 13
  water cycle 26
auroras 32
Australia 16
autumn 11

B

bacteria 15
Baikal, Lake 27
barite 18, *18*
basalt 18, 21
bathyscaphes 30, *30*
Bay of Fundy, Canada 31
black smokers 31, *31*
braiding 27

C

calcite 18, *18*
calcium 9
California, USA 21, 25
Cambrian Period 15, *15*
Canada 31

canyons, submarine 30, *30*
carbon dioxide 22, 32
Carboniferous Period 15
Caribbean 35
caves 19
chalk 19
Challenger Deep 30
chemicals, composition of the Earth 9
chimneys, undersea 31
China 24
cirques 28
cirrostratus clouds 33
cirrus clouds 33
clay 19
climate **12–13**, *12*
clouds 13, 14, 26, 33, *33*, 34
Colombia, USA 12
comets 15
composition of the Earth 9, *9*
cone volcanoes 23, *23*
continental shelf 30, *30*
continental slope 30, *30*
continents 8, **16-17**
  climate 12
  continental drift 16–17
  formation 14
core 8, 14
Crater Lake 23, *23*
craters, volcanoes 23
Cretaceous Period 15
crevasses 28
crust 8, 9, 14, 21
crystals
  ice 33
  rocks 18
  snowflakes 29
cumulonimbus clouds 33, *33*
cumulus clouds 33, *33*
cyclones 33

D

Dallol, Ethiopia 12
Darling, River 26, *26*
dating rocks 14, 15
day and night 10, *10*
Dead Sea 31
deltas 27, *27*
depressions, weather 33, 35
deserts 13, 19
Devonian Period 15, *15*
diameter of the Earth 9
diamonds 18, 19
dinosaurs 17

E

earthquakes 8, 16, **24–25**

earthquakes (*continued*)
  fault block mountains 20, *20*, 21, *21*
  hypocentre 24, *24*
  measuring 25
  metamorphic rocks 18
  tidal waves 25
  zones 25, *25*
Ecuador 12
Elbrus, Mount 20, *20*
electricity, thunderstorms 34
elements 9, 14
emeralds 19
epicentre, earthquakes 24, *24*
Equator 9, 10, 12, 33
Erie, Lake 27, *27*
erosion 19
eruptions, volcanoes 22–23, *22*
Ethiopia 12
Europe 8, 16, 17, 27, 28
Everest, Mount 21, *21*, 22
exosphere 32, *32*

F

fault block mountains 20, *20*, 21
faults 25
Flora, hurricane 35
fold mountains 20, 21
forests 13
formation of the Earth 14, *14*
fossils 14, 15, *15*, 17
fronts, weather 35, *35*
frost, erosion 19, *19*
fumaroles 23, *23*

G

galena 18, *18*
gases
  atmosphere 8, 32
  global warming 13
gems 18, 19
geodes 18
geology 15
George V Island 32
geysers 23, *23*
glaciers **28–29**, *28*
global warming 12, 13
Gondwanaland 16, *16*
gravity 10, 14, 31
Great Lakes 27, *27*
greenhouse effect 13, *13*
gypsum 18, *18*

H

hailstorm 35
Hawaii 21, 23
helium 32
Himalayas, Mountains 21, *21*
horst 20
Hubbard Glacier 28
Huron, Lake 27, *27*
hurricanes 32, 34, 35, *35*
  Flora 35
hydrogen 14
hydrothermal vents 31, *31*
hypocentre, earthquakes 24, *24*

I

ice **28-29**
  comets 15
  firmification 28
  glaciers 28
  global warming 12
  ice sheets 26, 29
  icebergs 29, *29*
  in clouds 33
ice ages 27, 28
Iceland 23
igneous rocks 18
India 16, 21, 35
Indian Ocean 30
iron 8, 9, 14
islands 23

J

Japan 24
Java 22
Jayakusama, Mount 20, *20*
Jurassic Period 15, *15*

K

K2, Mount 21
Kanchenjunga, Mount 21
Kilimanjaro, Mount 20, *20*
Kobe 24
Krakatoa 22
krypton 32

L

lakes 23, 26, 27
  Baikal 27
  Crater 23, *23*
  Erie 27, *27*
  Huron 27, *27*
  Michigan 27, *27*
  Ontario 27, *27*
  oxbows 27
  Superior 27, *27*
Lambert–Fisher Ice Passage 28

The publishers would like to thank the
following artists who have contributed to this book:
Kuo Kang Chen, Chris Forsey, Jeremy Gower, Alan Hancocks, Rob Jakeway,
Kevin Maddison, Maltings, Janos Marffy, Guy Smith, Rudi Vizi, Steve Weston

The publishers wish to thank the following sources for the photographs used in this book:
AFP: p24 b/l

All other photographs are from:
Corel, DigitalSTOCK, PhotoDisc